Kangaroos

Julie Murray

Abdo
Kids

I LIKE ANIMALS!

abdopublishing.com

Published by Abdo Kids, a division of ABDO, PO Box 398166, Minneapolis, Minnesota 55439.
Copyright © 2017 by Abdo Consulting Group, Inc. International copyrights reserved in all countries.
No part of this book may be reproduced in any form without written permission from the publisher.

Printed in the United States of America, North Mankato, Minnesota.

102016

012017

 THIS BOOK CONTAINS
RECYCLED MATERIALS

Photo Credits: iStock, Shutterstock

Production Contributors: Teddy Borth, Jennie Forsberg, Grace Hansen

Design Contributors: Christina Doffing, Candice Keimig, Dorothy Toth

Publisher's Cataloging in Publication Data

Names: Murray, Julie, author.

Title: Kangaroos / by Julie Murray.

Description: Minneapolis, Minnesota : Abdo Kids, 2017 | Series: I like animals! |
    Includes bibliographical references and index.

Identifiers: LCCN 2016943924 | ISBN 9781680809053 (lib. bdg.) |
    ISBN 9781680796155 (ebook) | ISBN 9781680796827 (Read-to-me ebook)

Subjects: LCSH: Kangaroos--Juvenile literature.

Classification: DDC 599.2--dc23

LC record available at http://lccn.loc.gov/2016943924

Table of Contents

Kangaroos

Kangaroos live in **Australia**.

They hop on two legs.

Their back legs are long.

Their front legs are short.

They have big feet.

They can hop fast.

They have long tails.

They use them to balance.

They have big ears.

They can hear well.

They have fur. It is brown, gray, or red.

brown

gray

red

15

They eat plants.

They eat grass, too.

A baby is called a joey.

It grows up in its mother's pouch. She keeps it safe.

Have you seen a kangaroo?

Some Kinds of Kangaroos

antilopine kangaroo

red kangaroo

eastern grey kangaroo

western grey kangaroo

Glossary

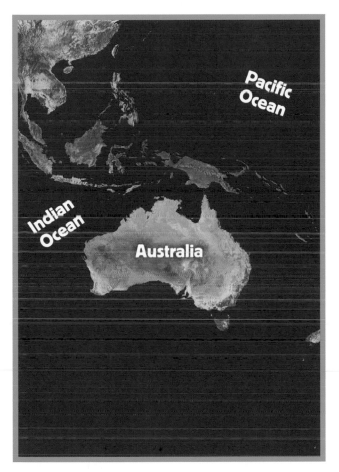

Australia
a continent between the Indian and Pacific oceans.

balance
even out weight to allow oneself to stay upright.

Index

abdokids.com

Use this code to log on to abdokids.com and access crafts, games, videos, and more!

Abdo Kids Code:
IKK9053